DATE DUE		

Punishment and Rehabilitation

CRIME, JUSTICE, AND PUNISHMENT

Punishment and Rehabilitation

Rose Blue and
Corinne J. Naden

Austin Sarat, GENERAL EDITOR

CHELSEA HOUSE PUBLISHERS
Philadelphia

Frontis: *Rehabilitation efforts like this group counseling session are designed to help inmates lead productive, law-abiding lives once they are released from prison.*

Chelsea House Publishers
Editor in Chief Sally Cheney
Director of Production Kim Shinners
Creative Manager Takeshi Takahashi
Manufacturing Manager Diann Grasse

Staff for PUNISHMENT AND REHABILITATION
Associate Editor Bill Conn
Production Assistant Jaimie Winkler
Picture Researcher Pat Burns
Cover and Series Designer Takeshi Takahashi
Layout 21st Century Publishing and Communications, Inc.

First Printing

1 3 5 7 9 8 6 4 2

The Chelsea House World Wide Web address is
http://www.chelseahouse.com

Library of Congress Cataloging-in-Publication Data

Blue, Rose.
    Punishment and rehabilitation / Rose Blue and
        Corinne J. Naden.
        p. cm. — (Crime, justice, and punishment)
Includes bibliographical references and index.
    ISBN 0-7910-4313-4
  1. Criminals—Rehabilitation—United States—Juvenile
literature. 2. Juvenile delinquents—Rehabilitation—
United States—Juvenile literature. 3. Punishment—
United States—Juvenile literature. 4. Criminal justice,
Administration of—Juvenile literature. [1. Punishment.
2. Criminals—Rehabilitation. 3. Juvenile delinquents—
Rehabilitation. 4. Criminal justice, Administration of.]
I. Naden, Corinne J. II. Title. III. Series.
HV9304 .B58 2000
364—dc21
                                        00-031648

Contents

CRIME, JUSTICE, AND PUNISHMENT

Fears and Fascinations:

An Introduction to Crime, Justice, and Punishment

By Austin Sarat

We live with crime and images of crime all around us. Crime evokes in most of us a deep aversion, a feeling of profound vulnerability, but it also evokes an equally deep fascination. Today, in major American cities the fear of crime is a major fact of life, some would say a disproportionate response to the realities of crime. Yet the fear of crime is real, palpable in the quickened steps and furtive glances of people walking down darkened streets. At the same time, we eagerly follow crime stories on television and in movies. We watch with a "who done it" curiosity, eager to see the illicit deed done, the investigation undertaken, the miscreant brought to justice and given his just deserts. On the streets the presence of crime is a reminder of our own vulnerability and the precariousness of our taken-for-granted rights and freedoms. On television and in the movies the crime story gives us a chance to probe our own darker motives, to ask "Is there a criminal within?" as well as to feel the collective satisfaction of seeing justice done.

Fear and fascination, these two poles of our engagement with crime, are, of course, only part of the story. Crime is, after all, a major social and legal problem, not just an issue of our individual psychology. Politicians today use our fear of, and fascination with, crime for political advantage. How we respond to crime, as well as to the political uses of the crime issue, tells us a lot about who we are as a people as well as what we value and what we tolerate. Is our response compassionate or severe? Do we seek to understand or to punish, to enact an angry vengeance or to rehabilitate and welcome the criminal back into our midst? The CRIME, JUSTICE, AND PUNISHMENT series is designed to explore these themes, to ask why we are fearful and fascinated, to probe the meanings and motivations of crimes and criminals and of our responses to them, and, finally, to ask what we can learn about ourselves and the society in which we live by examining our responses to crime.

Crime is always a challenge to the prevailing normative order and a test of the values and commitments of law-abiding people. It is sometimes a Raskolnikov-like act of defiance, an assertion of the unwillingness of some to live according to the rules of conduct laid out by organized society. In this sense, crime marks the limits of the law and reminds us of law's all-too-regular failures. Yet sometimes there is more desperation than defiance in criminal acts; sometimes they signal a deep pathology or need in the criminal. To confront crime is thus also to come face-to-face with the reality of social difference, of class privilege and extreme deprivation, of race and racism, of children neglected, abandoned, or abused whose response is to enact on others what they have experienced themselves. And occasionally crime, or what is labeled a criminal act, represents a call for justice, an appeal to a higher moral order against the inadequacies of existing law.

Figuring out the meaning of crime and the motivations of criminals and whether crime arises from defiance, desperation, or the appeal for justice is never an easy task. The motivations and meanings of crime are as varied as are the persons who engage in criminal conduct. They are as mysterious as any of the mysteries of the human soul. Yet the desire to know the secrets of crime and the criminal is a strong one, for in that knowledge may lie one step on the road to protection, if not an assurance of one's own personal safety. Nonetheless, as strong as that desire may be, there is no available technology that can allow us to know the whys of crime with much confidence, let alone a scientific certainty. We can, however, capture something about crime by studying the defiance, desperation, and quest for justice that may be associated with it. Books in the CRIME, JUSTICE, AND PUNISHMENT series will take up that challenge. They tell stories of crime and criminals, some famous, most not, some glamorous and exciting, most mundane and commonplace.

This series will, in addition, take a sober look at American criminal justice, at the procedures through which we investigate crimes and identify criminals, at the institutions in which innocence or guilt is determined. In these procedures and institutions we confront the thrill of the chase as well as the challenge of protecting the rights of those who defy our laws. It is through the efficiency and dedication of law enforcement that we might capture the criminal; it is in the rare instances of their corruption or brutality that we feel perhaps our deepest betrayal. Police, prosecutors, defense lawyers, judges, and jurors administer criminal justice and in their daily actions give substance to the guarantees of the Bill of Rights. What is an adversarial system of justice? How does it work? Why do we have it? Books in the CRIME, JUSTICE, AND PUNISHMENT series will examine the thrill of the chase as we seek to capture the criminal. They will also reveal the drama and majesty of the criminal trial as well as the day-to-day reality of a criminal justice system in which trials are the exception and negotiated pleas of guilty are the rule.

When the trial is over or the plea has been entered, when we have separated the innocent from the guilty, the moment of punishment has arrived. The injunction to punish the guilty, to respond to pain inflicted by inflicting pain, is as old as civilization itself. "An eye for an eye and a tooth for a tooth" is a biblical reminder that punishment must measure pain for pain. But our response to the criminal must be better than and different from the crime itself. The biblical admonition, along with the constitutional prohibition of "cruel and unusual punishment," signals that we seek to punish justly and to be just not only in the determination of who can and should be punished, but in how we punish as well. But neither reminder tells us what to do with the wrongdoer. Do we rape the rapist, or burn the home of the arsonist? Surely justice and decency say no. But, if not, then how can and should we punish? In a world in which punishment is neither identical to the crime nor an automatic response to it, choices must be made and we must make them. Books in the CRIME, JUSTICE, AND PUNISHMENT series will examine those choices and the practices, and politics, of punishment. How do we punish and why do we punish as we do? What can we learn about the rationality and appropriateness of today's responses to crime by examining our past and its responses? What works? Is there, and can there be, a just measure of pain?

CRIME, JUSTICE, AND PUNISHMENT brings together books on some of the great themes of human social life. The books in this series capture our fear and fascination with crime and examine our responses to it. They remind us of the deadly seriousness of these subjects. They bring together themes in law, literature, and popular culture to challenge us to think again, to think anew, about subjects that go to the heart of who we are and how we can and will live together.

*   *   *   *   *

Punishment, as Friedrich Nietzsche reminds us, helps make us who we are and constitutes us as particular kinds of people. The person constituted by punishment is watchful, on guard, fearful, even if never directly subject to the particular pains of state imposed punishment. One of the primary achievements of punishment, to use Nietzsche's vivid phrase, "is to breed an animal with the right to make promises," that is, to induce in us a sense of responsibility, a desire and an ability to take and properly discharge our social obligations. Dutiful individuals, guilt ridden, morally burdened—these are the creatures that punishment demands, creatures worthy of being punished.

Punishment helps make us who we are through the complex juridical mechanisms which put it in motion as well as the moral tenets and legal doctrines which legitimate it. Here too we can see the centrality of responsibility. The state will only punish persons whose "deviant" acts can be said to be a product of consciousness and will, persons who "could have done otherwise." As the famous jurist William Blackstone put it, "to constitute a crime against human laws, there must be, first, a vicious will, and, secondly, an unlawful act consequent upon such vicious will." Thus the apparatus of punishment depends upon a belief in individual responsibility and conceptions of will that represses or forgets its "uncertain, divided, and opaque" character.

In addition, because most citizens are not, and will not be, directly subjected to the state's penal apparatus, punishment creates a challenge for representation which is deepened to the point of crisis when the punishment is death. Punishment lives in images conveyed, in lessons taught, in repressed memories, in horrible imaginings. Some of its horror and controlling power is, in fact, a result of its fearful invisibility. It may very well be, however, that the more punishment is hidden, the more power it has to colonize our imaginative life. We watch; we seek an image of punishment; we become particular kinds of spectators, anticipating a glimpse, at least a partial uncovering of the apparatus of state discipline. Thus public fascination with "crime and criminal justice never flags."

This book speaks directly to this fascination, directing its readers to consider the capacity of punishment to change persons and behavior. It speaks to critical contemporary debates as well as venerable questions in vivid and interesting prose. It charts where we as a society are and highlights the questions which we will have to address in the immediate future, questions about what we want to do with our system of criminal punishment.

CRIME AND PUNISHMENT IN THE UNITED STATES

Crimes are defined by the criminal and penal codes of a particular country or state. These codes tell citizens what is legal or illegal. However, definitions of crime are not universal—what may be legal in one country or state may be illegal in another. Murder, for example, is recognized as a crime in most parts of the world, but abortion is a crime in some places and not in others.

The criminal code in the United States has evolved over centuries, and has its origins in the English criminal law system. Neither country has ever instituted a nationwide criminal code; the U.S. code varies from state to state. In general, however, all states distinguish between two types of crimes: felonies and misdemeanors. Felonies, such as murder and armed robbery, are punishable by death or prison terms longer than one year. Misdemeanors are lesser offenses, such as too many unpaid parking tickets, and are punishable by fines, jail terms of less than a year, and/or community service.

Almost everyone would agree that crimes, especially felonies, should be punished. However, what is not as readily agreed upon is what the goal of that punishment should be. This book examines one of the goals of punishment: rehabilitation. "Rehabilitation" means to restore, to bring back to its former good quality. Just as a talented carpenter may try to restore a battered piece of furniture to its former elegance, so rehabilitation in the U.S. prison system tries to restore people, to bring them back to being the law-abiding citizens they were before they committed crimes.

Almost everyone would also agree that we should work to prevent crime. Some law enforcement officials believe the best way to do that is through rehabilitation. They believe it should be the main goal of punishment; criminals should not be put in jail simply to serve time, but to change their ways so they don't commit crimes again. Others disagree and say that punishment itself is what stops crime. They don't believe that rehabilitation prevents future crimes.

In primitive societies, punishment was often determined by the victim of the crime, or the victim's family. This practice often meant that the punishment had very little relationship to the crime committed, and the goal of that punishment was almost always revenge. An angry farmer might order you beheaded for stealing a handful of wheat! But as time went on, the idea of appropriate punishment took shape in the form of "an eye for an eye." Of course, this could be rather severe, too. If you stole an apple with your right hand, you might not only lose the apple, but your hand as well! Harsh physical punishment was common.

Gradually, however, society began to object to the idea of punishment that caused physical pain. People began to recognize that one punishment was not appropriate for all crimes; there may be circumstances and conditions that should be taken into account when judging the punishment for a crime.

Our modern theories of crime and punishment have their roots in the humanitarian movement that began in the 18th century. The humanitarian movement taught that an individual, even a criminal, has dignity and basic human rights. It claimed that lawbreakers were products of society and could not be held totally and solely responsible for their actions. This movement led to prison reforms, to a studies of types of criminals, and to the view that habitual crime should be treated as disease.

Since then, government leaders, philosophers, and prison officials have debated over the goals of punishment. Although there is some disagreement and confusion over terms and definitions, in general there are four objectives of punishment in the United States: retribution, deterrence, incapacitation, and rehabilitation.

The idea behind retribution is that if you cause pain to someone, a measure of pain should be inflicted upon you. However, in a just society there should be a relationship between the seriousness of the crime and the severity of the punishment. In other words, you don't go to jail for ten years if your crime is stealing a loaf of bread.

As one of the goals of punishment, retribution may be an end in itself; the criminal repays the debt he incurred when he committed the crime by suffering under the terms of his punishment. However, it may be argued that retribution is an educating process and will deter future crime, since the criminal will not want to suffer the same punishment again. And finally, retribution may also be viewed as a way to satisfy the victims of crime in some way. An unsatisfied crime victim might decide to take the law into his or her own hands.

Deterrence is what punishment is all about, of course —stopping the behavior that brought on the crime. The theory of deterrence isn't concerned with the future of the criminal, except in a subtle way by inflicting punishment that causes some form of pain and shows

Deterrence prevents crime by instilling the fear of additional punishment in the criminal. Punishments that use physical pain, like the water torture practiced at Sing Sing prison in the 19th century, have since been replaced by more humane and constructive punishments.

that the person's behavior was wrong. Deterrence is concerned with stopping the offending behavior immediately. Society assumes that the person who has committed the offense wants to avoid the pain of future punishment, and will therefore not commit another crime. For instance, one form of deterrence is taking away a person's driving license after being convicted for driving while intoxicated (DWI). This assumes that the offender is rational and will not want to have the same punishment inflicted again. It also assumes that someone else with a tendency to drive while drinking will not want to suffer the same punishment. Studies show that this kind of deterrence does have at least a temporary effect on society as a whole. However, it is often difficult to prove if deterrence is, in fact, the real cause of behavioral changes in society.

Incapacitation is a simple, straightforward, ancient idea: If you execute criminals or put them behind bars —in olden times they were often banished from society, a fairly certain death sentence—they can't commit more crimes. And, with the exception of the criminal perhaps, this approach makes everyone happy. Furthermore, one can't argue with the fact that of all the objectives of punishment, this is the one that we know for certain works! Except for the fairly rare successful prison break, the criminal in jail is not out on the streets threatening the law-abiding public.

In practice, this theory of punishment is as limited as the criminal's prison sentence. Only habitual criminals or criminals who have been sentenced for some particularly horrendous deeds are incapacitated for life. Charles Manson is a case in point. In August 1969, he led a gang of frenzied young people on a savage murder spree in southern California. Actress Sharon Tate and several of her friends were killed. Manson and others went to prison. Each time he has become eligible for parole, he has been turned down. It is likely that Manson will remain incapacitated as long as he lives. However, the vast majority of criminals are eventually released from prison, and are free to commit more crimes.

Rehabilitation is the newest of the four theories of punishment. This theory claims that the punishment itself will reform the offender. After the proscribed time in prison, he or she will be prepared to become a productive, law-abiding member of society once again.

This idea began to take hold in the 19th century

and was seen by many as a more humane and lenient view of the criminal. Rehabilitation, however, did not always mean a lighter than normal sentence. Sometimes it actually meant a longer time behind bars, during which time the criminal underwent some sort of treatment or training. Sometimes it meant release on probation instead of prison time. In many jurisdictions, rehabilitation took the form of prison sentences that were unspecified as to time. If the offender showed signs of reform, he or she might be released; if not, the offender stayed in prison.

Although the goals of punishment stand by themselves, we have a tendency to group the first three—retribution, deterrence, and incapacitation—as the benefits of being "tough on crime." And we tend to regard rehabilitation, at least by some critics, as a liberal or moral response.

Much of the way we look at crime and criminals depends on what is going on around us. That's why there have been rises and falls, ups and downs in how we feel about rehabilitation as a crime deterrent.

In the late 18th and early 19th centuries, criminals were viewed as a moral problem that had to be dealt with strictly. Lawbreakers were wayward citizens—sinners, in fact. It was thought that they must be made to "see the light," and going to prison could do that. Different groups accomplished this goal in different ways. The Quakers in Pennsylvania isolated the offender, leaving him no choice but to meditate on his sins. U.S. prison officials had another way. They thought that hard work and strict discipline would reform the criminal.

Let's look at Sing Sing Correctional Facility as an example. Located in Ossining, New York, 33 miles north of New York City on the Hudson River, Sing Sing first became operational in the 1820s. Officials felt that hard work and discipline would change a criminal's ways. A new inmate was placed in a cell that was 3 1/2 feet wide, not quite 7 feet long, and about 6 1/2 feet

high. (Measure that space on your floor and see how small it is!) The inmates were sent to work in the nearby rock quarry. The theory was that if the punishment was tougher than the inmates, they would learn the evil of their ways.

As time passed, however, society's views about crime and criminals underwent another change. The offender was seen not as a lost sinner, but as a sick human being who could, and should, be cured. Criminal behavior began to be viewed more as an addiction, like gambling or alcohol.

Rehabilitation first gained popularity as a goal of punishment in the 19th century. Today, prisons offer education and job training to inmates in the hope that they will not return to a life of crime after they are released from prison.

Although prisoners no longer suffer physical punishments, their freedom is taken away when they are incarcerated. This tiny cell at the Sing Sing Correctional Facility shows just how harsh the living conditions in prison really are.

The attitude of regarding the criminal as having a sick mind continued into the good feeling era of the post-World War II years. People in the United States were optimistic that rehabilitation would be the answer to the rising crime rate. Work programs, in-jail therapy sessions, indeterminate sentences, and halfway houses eased the return to a law-abiding life.

But, as always, the world changes. By the 1970s, people were not quite so sure that rehabilitation was really the answer to reforming criminals. Why? For one thing, no one had demonstrated to the public's satisfaction that officials had a workable system of rehabilitation. Sometimes it worked with one criminal; lots of times it didn't. For another thing, the crime rate was growing. There was little doubt that American society was becoming more violent. Was it the easy availability of guns? Was it increased drug use? Was it the abundance of violence on TV and in the movies? Was it all these things?

Today, as always, different theories about rehabilitation and its place in the punishment process are in conflict. There is no doubt that the great optimism about rehabilitation has been dampened somewhat. Most people in law enforcement today feel that all punishment can accomplish is deterrence, or the more certain effect—incapacitation.

THROW AWAY THE KEY?

Since modern law enforcement has called the merits of rehabilitation into question, the "tough on crime" policies of retribution, incapacitation and deterrence seem to stand alone as the only goals of punishment. But if the answer to lowering the crime rate is to get tough, then it follows that we are going to have to put more and more people in jail for longer and longer periods. Is this solution possible, and if so, is it affordable?

As was discussed in the previous chapter, incapacitation reduces crime by keeping a criminal in jail, and incapable of committing another crime. In addition, jail is meant to be a deterrent. It teaches the offender the consequences of his crimes, which are a loss of freedom and difficult living conditions;

As the debate over the merits of rehabilitation rages, the crime rate in the United States continues to rise. If retribution, incapacitation, and deterrence continue as the only goals of punishment, more and more prisons like this one in Colorado will have to be built at the taxpayers' expense.

this punishment is supposed to be harsh enough to make the offender want to avoid it in the future, thus preventing future crimes as well.

However, if incapacitation and deterrence worked, our jails would be filled with first-time offenders. Unfortunately, they are not. Our jails have become revolving doors for some; for others, their third conviction lands them behind bars for the rest of their lives. And keeping more people in prison for longer periods is a very expensive process.

In 1995, for example, Governor George Pataki wanted New York State to build more prisons. The people might have been in favor, but not at the expense of social services, which would have been cut back if the prison bill passed. Prisons just cost too much – an average of $55,000 for each new cell! It costs about $22,000 a year to keep one inmate incarcerated. And the older he or she gets, the longer he or she stays behind bars, the more expensive the upkeep becomes. Overall, the U.S. prison system costs about $12 billion a year to operate!

Let's return to Sing Sing Correctional Facility for an example of the strengths and weaknesses of a typical prison system with incapacitation and deterrence as its primary goals. This maximum security prison operates on a yearly budget of $41 million. It employs about 1,000 people to tend to a male inmate population of about 2,300. Some 600 female inmates are housed in Bedford Hills and Taconic Correctional Facility, both part of the Sing Sing complex.

Although maximum security, about 500 of Sing Sing's prisoners are medium security risks. They are nearing parole or have behaved well enough to be less scrutinized. These inmates live behind bars, but in dormitories rather than cells, and have some limited freedom to move about their buildings.

Using Sing Sing's inmate population as typical of the state, slightly more than half are serving time for violent felonies, 54 percent of whom are on their second felony arrest. Forty-seven percent of inmates are in jail for drug offenses; these drug offense charges have inflated the prison rate over the past two decades. The average minimum sentence at Sing Sing is 42 months. Nearly 70 percent of its felons are from New York City, having been shipped "up the river" to serve time.

A majority of those behind bars in Sing Sing are African American or Hispanic. Some people use such statistics to indicate that minorities are somehow more "criminal" than whites. But these figures are far more indicative of poor educational and social backgrounds than of inherent racial characteristics. In addition, there have long been charges that African Americans and Hispanics are "picked up" on suspicion of crimes without justification far more often than whites, and that once charged their sentences are more harsh. In 1999, Governor Christine Whitman of New Jersey fired the head of the state's troopers after receiving numerous complaints by minorities that the police were stopping them on the highways more often than whites and without just cause. This phenomenon is known as racial profiling.

Sing Sing is run by the Superintendent, who reports to the Commissioner of Corrections at the state capitol in Albany, New York. The Superintendent's deputies include the Deputy Superintendent of Security, who is responsible for all security and discipline throughout the prison. In addition, a support staff includes Personnel, Fiscal Administration, Food Service, Medical and Dental Services, and Plant Operations and Maintenance.

Food Service, with its staff of nine security officers, nine civilian workers, and 22 inmates, operates two kitchens, and four separate dining rooms, called mess halls. They prepare more than 6,000 meals daily. Medical and Dental Services operates a 23-bed ward, a full dental service, and a psychiatric unit. The professional medical staff of 36 is assisted by "civilian" doctors in all specialties.

Modern prisons like Sing Sing are highly structured and efficient: when new prisoners arrive at the facility, they are evaluated for problems like drug addiction or violent personalities. A counselor and specialized program are then assigned to each prisoner according to their needs.

A new inmate enters Sing Sing via the reception gallery where he will spend the first five days. During that time, a program is set up for his stay in prison. If he has a history of violence, he will be placed in a special program. If he has a drug or alcohol problem, he goes into the Substance Abuse Program. If he can't read or write at an eighth grade level, he must attend school. Sing Sing has a computer lab, a general library, and a law library, in addition to college program courses.

The new inmate gets a counselor who will see him at least four times a year. Religious services are also offered. He also will be assigned to a vocational program, such as welding, barbering, or carpentry. Some of these programs allow the prisoner to earn 45 cents to $1.55 per day. However, the higher wages are paid only to those who have earned a high school equivalency diploma.

If the Sing Sing inmate does not follow his program, he's in more trouble than just being in prison. For one thing, when it comes time for parole, he may be denied. Penalties depend on the infraction. Minor offenses may mean only a "dressing down" by the security officer, or confinement to the cell and/or loss of privileges. For major infractions, the inmate may be confined to his cell for a long period, or may go to the "Box," a special unit outside the main cell compound for those whose behavior has caused the loss of all privileges for a specified time.

All in all, this schedule may not seem too much harder than, perhaps, a strict military school. But probably the Sing Sing inmates who walk outside for exercise and look up at the high cement wall with its barbed-wire-topped anchor fencing and state-of-the-art surveillance equipment would disagree.

Prison by whatever name is, after all, prison.

Unless, of course, it is super-max, the state-of-the art, twenty-first-century answer to incapacitation. These new prisons are designed not just to isolate the criminal from society, as did the Pennsylvania Quakers in the late 1700s and early 1800s, but to isolate him from other criminals as well.

Until it was closed in 1963, Alcatraz, the prison known as The Rock in San Francisco Bay, California, was considered the most secure of the all U.S. prisons. Only the most violent and dangerous felons in the country were sent there. After Alcatraz, that distinction fell to Marion prison in Illinois. Now Marion has lost its title to the federal facility in Florence, Colorado, opened in 1995. These super-max prisons are designed to keep prisoners virtually by themselves virtually all of the time. They are alone in their cells 23 hours a day. They eat there, they sleep there, they do everything there. By law, they are allowed to exercise one hour daily. That's it.

These truly are people the law has given up on. Using high technology to solve security and other concerns, the super-max prison takes the warehousing of criminals to its logical conclusion. It solves overcrowding by erasing practically all human contact among inmates. Psychologists say, however, that such extreme isolation will surely create psychological problems in these prisoners. However, the super-max's prime concern is keeping prisoners isolated, not on what will happen to them if and when they get out. Obviously, there is no attempt at or hope for rehabilitation in the super-max.

Today, more than 1.8 million Americans are in prison. That's an amazing figure when you consider that it amounts to about one out of every 150 people. If the population of your town is 20,000, for instance, 133 of your neighbors would be behind bars! This statistic also puts the United States at the top of the list of nations with the most citizens in prison.

Does this mean that there is a higher crime rate in the United States than in other countries? No, it doesn't. However, those figures do say some things about crime in America.

It is true that the number of Americans behind bars has doubled since 1985. However, the U.S. crime rate has remained remarkably stable since the 1970s and has been falling slightly since 1992. Compared with other industrialized countries, U.S. rates are highest only for homicide and attempted burglary.

How did the United States become the murder capital of the world? Officials point to the number of firearms on our streets. In countries where guns are not so easy to get, a robber, for instance, may use his fists instead of a gun in a fight. In America, he will likely shoot.

But why do we have so many people in jail? Authorities point out two major reasons: (1) we lock up people more often and for longer sentences for lesser crimes than we used to, and (2) the drug problem. Most inmates in

As the number of Americans behind bars continues to grow, so does the problem of overcrowding in prisons. Many critics argue that this problem would be solved by offering rehabilitation programs, rather than prison sentences, to non-violent drug offenders.

the United States are in prison on drug charges. Since 1980, drug-related sentences in state prisons have gone up by 29 percent.

Additionally, Americans have become increasingly angry over repeat offenses of violent crimes. Every day on television we see someone shot or stabbed or assaulted, and we are even afraid of being crime victims in broad daylight. We want criminals off our streets. We want to feel safe. And we think that building more prisons, and keeping inmates in longer will solve the problem.

From this anger and fear come demands to bring back the death penalty in states where it was abolished, to institute a "no parole" policy, and to tell the habitual offender, "three strikes and you're out." For all these reasons, our prison population is growing.

The movement to abolish parole began in the late 1970s after studies suggested that early release from prison for good conduct did not reduce repeat offenses. Jack King, of the National Association of Criminal Defense Lawyers (NSCDL), is against the no-parole law. In an interview for this book, he said, "Parole is a good idea for prisoners who are well behaved and for those who are not well behaved. Why? Because parole gives something for people to shoot for. If there's no incentive, such as parole, why behave? That's one of the reasons correction officers are in favor of parole. It helps to keep the offenders in line. A correction officer feels his job is more dangerous when he must deal with inmates who know they have no chance to get out."

In 1984, the federal government abolished parole in sentencing offenders. King believes this just caused more of a mess. "Here's what can happen," he said. "The Hobbs Act is a federal law against interfering with interstate commerce. Suppose a kid snatches a purse along the southern border of Virginia and runs over into North Carolina? He's not only snatched a purse, which is, we'll say, his first crime and a relatively minor offense, but he has just interfered with interstate commerce! Therefore,

Kidnapper Richard Allen Davis is an example of the problems plaguing the parole policies in the United States. After California dropped its parole policy, the state had no choice but to release Davis since he had served his time. Shortly after being released, he murdered a young girl.

the judge who sentences him has no leeway at all. He can't, perhaps, sentence the kid to community work or whatever. No, he must send him to jail. The kid could get 20 years for purse snatching with no chance of parole!"

Of course, that's not what the no-parole law was meant to do at all. It was meant to stop such criminals as kidnapper Richard Allen Davis, for instance. He was rejected six times by the California parole board, who believed he was too dangerous to leave prison. But when California dropped its parole policy, Davis was automatically released since he had served the required time. In a few months, he murdered a 13-year-old girl.

In 1999, New York State proposed to join the 15 other states that have eliminated their parole boards. Does it work? Experts say that there are no statistics to show that taking away parole has lowered the crime rate in any state. There is one exception, of course. If a kidnapper, for instance, has to serve his full 20-year sentence instead of getting out in 10, he can't be kidnapping for those extra 10 years.

Three states—Connecticut, Colorado, and Florida—that took parole off their books have put it back on. The reason? Eliminating parole did not increase the amount of time that criminals served. Why? Because prisons became so crowded that those nearing parole had to be let out early anyway!

So, what is the answer? Pro-punishment advocates believe the answer is more prisons. Build more prisons, make prisoners serve their full terms. That will keep the streets safe.

In the search for safer streets, the "three strikes and you're out" policy has caught the public's attention. The idea is to increase the prison sentence for the second offense and make it life without parole for the third. This seems like a good idea. Time and again we read stories of rapists, for instance, who get out of jail only to rape again. This wouldn't happen with the three strikes policy. Wouldn't it get violent criminals off the streets?

Again, in theory, yes. The trouble is, like most theories, real life has a way of skewing the results. In California, for instance, which has a very broad and very strict "three strikes" policy, very few of those put in jail for the third offense are violent criminals. The policy is more apt to snare the nonviolent offenders.

Michael Garcia's story illustrates the problem with the three strikes policy. Garcia stole about $7-worth of meat from a grocery story. He was out of work and hungry. He'd committed two crimes before, both related to his heroin habit, but no violence was involved and the money stolen was small. Counselors think Garcia should have been put in a drug rehab program. Instead, he faces life in prison for his third offense.

But even if the three strikes policy can be made to work as it is intended, the cost will be staggering. It's true we want violent criminals in jail, but how will we pay for them?

Opponents to the three strikes policy say that we shouldn't pay for them at all, and believe that building more prisons won't reduce crime. They believe that we must reduce the prison population, not add to it. For one thing, experts in the field of law enforcement say that whether rehabilitation works or not, the truth is that many offenders find prison to be a criminal finishing school of sorts. If they didn't know how to be a hardened criminal when they went in, they certainly will have learned to be by the time they come out.

Other experts argue for weeding out the nonviolent or mentally ill of the prison population, and putting them in rehabilitation programs. In addition, they believe the availability of surveillance equipment can permit some inmates to be free under supervision, and that we should be putting money into existing rehab programs and making them work. These experts believe that if these goals are accomplished, people will spend less time in prison. Even more important, the programs will reduce the rate of repeat crimes, which is good for the offender and the American citizen who fears for his or her safety on the street.

Some solutions to the problems inherent in the three strikes policy include fair and clear sentencing, and options for courts to hand out sentences that fit the crime. Look at these figures from a recent year: some 1,800 people were in federal prisons for murder. They served an average of 4 1/2 years. More than 12,000 first-time, nonviolent drug offenders were also behind bars. They served an average of 6 1/2 years. Some officials say that doesn't make sense.

Probation, that period following release from prison, has not worked very well in the United States. It doesn't put people back into productive lives and it doesn't cut down on repeat offenders. On average in the 1990s, about three million people were on probation during any one year. They were supposed to report at specified periods to a probation officer assigned to oversee their activities, keep them on the straight and narrow, and help them to find work. However, some officials claim there are far too few probation officers. The system doesn't protect the public and it doesn't help the offender. Spending money to train more probation officers may improve this system.

Day reporting centers could provide scheduled activities and programs to put some offenders back into society. Halfway houses, where offenders live and pay rent, could provide a transition between prison and freedom. Drug treatment centers will reduce the prison population and make our streets safer

Some nonviolent offenders don't need prison at all. Why not sentence them to community service, to cleaning up streets and public parks, instead of sitting behind bars?

All these ideas have been tried to some degree or another in the United States. Do the results support the idea of rehabilitation as our main goal in the prison system, or do they point the way toward even longer prison sentences? The answers are not clear.

However, those who call for greater emphasis on rehabilitation insist that putting more money and know-how into non-prison programs will accomplish some very important goals: jails will be populated only with violent prisoners and those deemed not able to be retrained. A large majority of the present U.S. prison population may once again become law-abiding citizens. If those things happen, the American taxpayer will be paying far less into the criminal system and, perhaps even more important, our streets will be a whole lot safer for everyone.

REHAB ON TRIAL

Rehabilitation efforts like this job training program are often not fully implemented, as critics of these programs claim that criminals are inherently bad and unable to change their ways. However, others view criminal behavior as a sickness that can be treated, and feel that rehabilitation programs are a key ingredient in the cure.

In 1956, audiences crowded the movie houses to see an unusual thriller called *The Bad Seed*. It had been adapted from a Broadway play by Maxwell Anderson and would be remade for television 30 years later. *The Bad Seed* struck horror into the hearts of many parents. It told the story of a young girl, played by Patty McCormack on stage and in film, who had "inherited evil genes," which eventually led her to cause the death of several people.

Is this possible? Could a person really be born bad? Nonsense, say some mental health professionals. It's more likely that the girl in *The Bad Seed* wasn't a bad kid at all, but a sick one. After all, today we have come to recognize that alcoholism, gambling, and drug addiction may be based on a physical problem, not the desire to get into or cause trouble. Genetic studies are starting to point in that direction. Alcoholism, for example, does seem to be more prevalent among children of alcoholics than in the general population. Are we born to be addicted?

If we meet a person suffering from diabetes or Parkinson's disease, we are sympathetic. We recognize that the person is sick. A long time ago, people with epilepsy, which can cause brain seizures, were thought to be insane or possessed by the devil. Now we know that the seizures, or convulsions, have a physical cause. We don't throw a person with epilepsy into prison for suffering a seizure even if someone else's property is destroyed in the process. In the same way, perhaps the criminal personality is an illness. A person should be treated, not punished; medically assisted, not incarcerated. If it's true that people who commit violent crimes, for instance, are not bad but sick, shouldn't we try to help instead of punish them for their crimes?

Others disagree with this rationale. Criminals often wait until they think it is safe to commit a crime. They don't mug someone in full view of a police car. They wait until the coast is clear. It's not at all like having a convulsion, which you can't control. If criminals can control their actions when it is to their advantage, why can't they control themselves and not commit the action at all? How sick can they be if they can wait until it's safe to act out their impulses? The opposite conclusion is drawn: they are bad, not sick. Punishment, not the doctor, is called for.

This debate has been going on for years, and it covers a very important issue. If criminals are viewed as evil, perhaps carrying the evil gene like the young girl in *The Bad Seed*, then there is probably very little we can do through rehabilitation. But if we look at criminals as basically ill, meaning they were somehow not socialized like most people into society, then there is a chance that we can teach a criminal to change his behavior.

The late Dr. Karl Menninger of the famed Menninger Psychiatric Hospital in Topeka, Kansas, felt that people who break the law should be treated more like we treat someone who has a disease. "The convicted offender," he said, "would be detained indefinitely pending a decision as to whether and how to reintroduce him successfully

into society." Menninger felt that once the criminal's personality is studied, all sorts of techniques, including psychotherapy, could be applied to adapt him or her successfully to the outside world.

But in many instances, we don't know how to treat the offender. We don't know how to adapt him or her successfully to the outside world. And sometimes the offense is so horrendous that people no longer care about a cure or rehabilitation. Cure the sex offender who preys on infants? Rehabilitate the child kidnapper who mutilates and kills? Even if we knew how, they say, we simply don't want to.

There's no doubt that enthusiasm for rehabilitation has waned in recent years, which is ironic because law enforcement officials are learning that rehabilitation does work, at least with some criminals and under some circumstances. The most successful efforts have been in drug rehabilitation and with violent juvenile offenders.

The majority of criminals with drug problems will commit crimes after their release from prison in order to support their habit. Although intensive drug rehabilitation has been shown to reduce the rate of recidivism, most prisons still emphasize incapacitation and deterrence over rehabilitation as the goal of punishment.

It is estimated that up to 60 percent of any prison population has a drug problem serious enough to need treatment. Obviously, if that problem is not taken care of in prison, it's going to continue after the inmate's release into society and probably result in more crime. Overall, the states are woefully poor in their rehabilitation efforts for drug addicts. For instance, California had an inmate population of more than 145,000 in 1996, and about 75 percent of them were drug users. Yet the state had only 400 drug treatment beds in the entire prison system! It has since added another 1,200 beds.

What works with drug treatment is intensive follow-up on the outside. The Key program in Delaware is a good example. Convicted criminals with a drug problem in Delaware are placed in a special unit within the main state prison for up to 15 months. From there, they leave prison and enter a transitional house for six months of aftercare.

The results are encouraging. Only 29 percent of those who completed both the in-prison and transitional programs were in trouble with the law after 18 months. Of those who took part in neither program, 70 percent were rearrested. Of those who went through the prison program only, 52 percent were rearrested.

The drug rehabilitation program in Delaware seems to work, but many rehabilitation efforts do not. Experts say it's because we really don't have a clear idea of what we're treating. We don't understand why criminals are the way they are and how they got that way. So, we often try things in a hit-or-miss way. "Get tough" rehabilitation efforts have been popular with the public but have proved to be largely ineffective and a waste of money and effort. These efforts include the "boot camp" prisons, electronic monitoring, and intensive supervision on the outside by parole officers. It's expensive—and it doesn't work well. Studies show that the get tough, boot camp approach, for instance, has very little effect on recidivism —the return to prison. The quick fix doesn't fix anything.

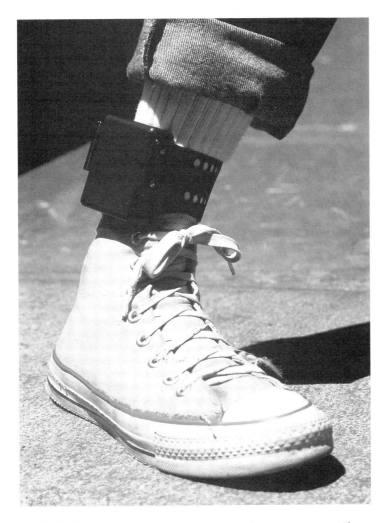

*Home incarceration with
electronic monitoring devices,
like this ankle bracelet, may help
reduce the overcrowded prison
population without risking an
increase in the crime rate.*

Rehabilitation programs have to be extensive. They
must have follow-up. There is little point in getting
a criminal off drugs and into job training if efforts aren't
made to get him a job when he's out of prison.

What about electronic monitoring? Overcrowding
and the cost of new prisons has led to the search for
ways to reduce the prison population without endan-
gering the public. One way is what some call "home
incarceration." There are different systems, but most
involve some sort of "bracelet" that attaches to the
ankle or wrist. The bracelet is programmed so that the

wearer cannot leave the house or grounds without sending a signal to the monitoring system. This keeps track of the parolee's whereabouts and reduces the prison population.

Some officials see home incarceration as practical means of rehabilitation, especially for nonviolent offenders. As the offender shows more and more promise of reforming, his "free area" may be extended until such time as he has been rehabilitated to the point where he can be left on his own.

The effectiveness of home incarceration is not yet fully recognized, although some critics say it is not as cost-effective as once thought and that it may be used to invade one's privacy. There are issues that will be dealt with as the practice grows more popular.

Some efforts at rehabilitating criminals, no matter what is tried, are blocked by a modern-day public attitude toward the rising crime rate. This attitude is often referred to as NIMBY—Not In My Back Yard. It points to the general fear about crime in the streets and in the neighborhood. Yes, people want criminals put away or reformed, but they don't want it done where they can see. Sometimes, of course, the fear is very real.

Such was the case in Hamilton Township, New Jersey, in 1993. Seven-year-old Megan Kanka lived there with her family. Jesse Timmendequas moved across the street. Jesse seemed nice enough, but Megan's parents probably would not have thought so if they had known that he was, in fact, a child sex offender. He had been released from the Adult Diagnostic and Treatment Center, a correctional facility for sex offenders in Avenel, New Jersey. No one in the neighborhood knew of his past.

One day, Jesse lured the trusting Megan into his home where he sexually molested and then killed her. Coupled with the devastating loss of her daughter and the fact that Megan was the third child to die so tragically during that year in Monmouth County, Megan's mother decided to do something. Maureen Kanka began a foundation in Megan's name and became a victims' rights activist. As a result of her tireless work and that of others, on October 31, 1994, Megan's Law was enacted.

Megan's Law says that sex offenders must register their whereabouts with police wherever they live. The police will then classify them according to risk. Neighbors will be notified of the offender's record. Any state not passing such a law risks losing federal funding.

The Megan Kanka Foundation works to see that community notification laws are observed and that background checks are carried out on ex-offenders. They encourage citizens to be on the lookout for suspicious behavior around children, especially in organized sports activities or other recreational areas.

One of the reasons that child molesters are so especially feared in communities is that, besides the obvious threat to children, therapy has not been very successful in dealing with these offenders. The rate of recidivism is very high. Recently, however, mental health professionals have reported encouraging results with a combination of behavioral and chemical therapy.

It is fairly certain that had Megan Kanka's parents known of their neighbor's background, he would not have been given the chance to be alone with the child. But some legalists have claimed that Megan's Law is unconstitutional. It violates a citizen's right to privacy and a personal life. If a person has served his or her time in prison, isn't notification of background a case of double jeopardy? Aren't we making the person pay for the same crime all over again? Aren't we in danger of encouraging vigilantism by exposing everyone's personal life to scrutiny?

Megan's Law has been challenged in court and has been upheld. In early 1999, a federal court in Philadelphia found that giving out personal information on sex offenders did not violate their privacy: " . . . sex offenders, like all criminals, have forfeited their rights to privacy regarding their crimes. They are therefore not protected if the police collect and circulate information about their addresses, jobs, crimes, education, physical appearance, auto registrations and license plate numbers."

The perceived rise in crime and the public's fear of violence have sometimes made rehabilitation efforts difficult as well. Americans have always tried to help the helpless, the homeless, the less fortunate. But somewhere along the way, we seem to have become less trusting, more hardened, perhaps just more fearful. Yes, we agree that rehabilitation centers may be the answer, but we are afraid to have them where we live. How about the homeless in our large urban centers? Shouldn't we build shelters to give them a place to sleep? Sure, we should, but where?

Not long ago a halfway house was built in a large eastern city for recovering drug addicts. The neighborhood wasn't happy. Addicts—recovering or not—might be a bad influence on the kids. They might even be dangerous. Lots of drug addicts are HIV positive. What about the spread of AIDS? One night the halfway house was bombed and destroyed. No one ever found out who was responsible.

But despite public fear and hostility, some community-based rehab programs do work. Founded in 1972, the Safer Foundation in Chicago is the largest community-based provider of employment services for ex-offenders in the United States. A professional staff of about 200 people in six locations helps ex-offenders to find good jobs, and also helps them to develop a frame of mind that keeps them employed and successful in life.

The Safer Foundation reaches many offenders while they are still in prison. Besides running a school to improve education, it helps to get the inmates ready for the

outside world in the job market. After release and entering the program, the ex-offender is assigned a case manager—called a lifeguard—who will follow him or her for one year after gaining employment.

There are no miracle cures at the Safer Foundation, but it does work. Annie is a typical example. She never held a regular job and was on welfare most of her life when she wasn't in prison for selling drugs. After her last release, however, she entered the Safer program and got her first paying job, with full benefits. After one year, she reported back to Safer because the company was cutting back and laying off its newest employees. Annie told Safer she had to have a job right away because she didn't want to miss a paycheck—this from

Educational and job training programs run by organizations like the Safer Foundation and Workfare give prisoners options other than returning to a life of crime after their release. The success of these programs makes rehabilitation seem like a viable goal of punishment.

a woman who until the past year had never earned even one paycheck her entire life!

Annie is back at work in a new job. She is proud of herself and confident of her ability to succeed. And she knows that Safer is there behind her.

Or how about Dan? He was in prison for assault. A foster child, a gang member, and a young man with a chip on his shoulder, Dan had an unmanageable temper. Before being released from prison, he went into Safer's Crossroads program. It is especially designed to help those offenders with special problems. In the Crossroads program, Dan earned his high school equivalency diploma and enrolled in a local school to study cooking, which he enjoyed.

Upon release from prison, Dan continued at the school. However, before he could graduate, the city closed down the school and Dan could not afford the tuition at another facility. The tough former gang member was in tears to have come so close to his chance at a promising future.

And miracles sometimes do happen. An anonymous donor paid the $4,000 tuition at another school for Dan. He graduated near the top of his class. Today, he is a productive citizen and the head chef at one of Chicago's top restaurants.

Chicago's Safer program is a large and successful operation, but smaller programs are also showing some promise. Workfare is gaining in popularity. Using ex-offenders to clean the streets or remove snow seems less threatening to the public than a halfway house down the street. The workers become a visible, constant presence, which makes them seem less fearful, just like any park or construction worker.

We seem to be at the halfway point with rehabilitation as the goal of punishment. We are learning that some rehab efforts do work, and if they do, we are one step closer to lowering the crime rate and making our streets safer. But we are also fearful as a society and angry over the violence in our midst. Many of us just want criminals out of the way— perhaps forever—and don't much care how we reach that goal.

WOMEN IN THE JAILHOUSE

It will probably come as no surprise to hear that women are different from men. Some of the crimes women commit are the same ones that land men in jail, some are not. And once convicted, women have different problems than men do in coping with a world behind bars.

Although the proportion of women in jail (51 out of 100,000) is far lower than for men (819 out of 100,000), the number of women entering U.S. prisons is growing at a faster rate than the number of men. In 1980, 4.1 percent of all women in the nation were in jail; in 1998, that figure was up to 6.4 percent.

About 43 percent of incarcerated women (compared to 12 percent of men) report a history of sexual abuse. Women are less likely than men to commit a violent

Female criminals are much different than their male counterparts: women generally commit non-violent crimes, have a low rate of recidivism, and respond well to minimal rehabilitation efforts.

49

crime such as murder or assault. However, those who do go to prison for violence are about twice as likely as men to have committed that crime against someone close to them. That person is often the husband or boyfriend who was physically or mentally abusive. The majority of women in prison have children under the age of 18. Women in prison are more likely than men to be drug addicts, to have mental illness, and to have been unemployed before they were jailed. Women are far more likely than men to stay out of prison once they get out.

These hard facts make some educators and leaders in the U.S. prison system sit up and take notice. If we take a good look at these facts, they say, we can make real changes in the prison system regarding women. And those changes might make a drastic change in the number of women who now fill up our jails.

Officials say that of all the hard facts listed above, two of them constitute very practical reasons for concentrating on rehabilitation for women offenders. The first reason is that most women in prison have children under the age of 18. If we can rehabilitate these offenders, if we can change their lives and turn them into law-abiding, productive citizens, chances are good that they will turn their children into law-abiding, productive citizens. Rehabilitation for women offenders may stop the cycle of crime that is often passed on from one generation to the other. The second reason is that women are more likely then men to stay out of jail once they get out. This trend works in favor of rehab for women. Even relatively small rehabilitation programs produce good results in a female prison population.

In general, women are less likely to commit crimes than men are, and far less likely to commit violent crimes. It's not that the female sex is any more virtuous than the male sex. The reasons lie more in the way men and women have been raised for centuries. Men have often been encouraged to fight, to use their fists instead of their reason to solve problems. Women are less likely to do so. Women, in general, tend to be less physically strong than men. Therefore, they have long sought means other than the physical to get out of a difficult situation.

But women can, and do, commit serious physical crimes like murder, assault, and manslaughter. Some go to jail for life for these offenses; some are executed. (Female juvenile offenders are discussed in Chapter 5.)

Some experts believe that women are treated more leniently in the court system than are men. That does not prove to be true, although women do tend to receive shorter sentences for the same crimes. The reason, however, is that women tend to have shorter criminal histories than men do. Prisons housing females have a much larger percentage of first-time offenders than those housing males. And when women get involved in large-scale criminal activity, they are less likely than men to play a vital role. In a big-time bank robbery, for instance, a female gang member is more likely to act as lookout than to be waving a gun in a teller's face.

Although many would argue that women offenders should be treated no differently than males—a criminal is a criminal, after all—there are some special circumstances, such as children, to consider with the female offender. Consider this: In 90 percent of the cases, children with fathers in prison are living with their mothers. But for children with mothers in prison, only 25 percent live with their fathers. That leaves an enormous number of children who are either cared for by relatives, by the state, or are perhaps shunted from foster home to foster home. A large percentage of those children grow up with emotional and behavioral problems, which some-times leads to crime, which often leads to prison . . . and the vicious cycle starts all over again.

About two-thirds of female prison inmates in any given U.S. facility are mothers. Some of their children are born behind bars. What happens to them? In the Bedford Hills, New York, correctional facility for women, part of the Sing Sing complex, children are cared for at the site. This form of rehabilitation helps to instill parenting skills in the female offender, who very often has none. In addition, the prison provides employment training in an effort to keep mother and child together when the woman is released. Many inmates are involved both in the program and in the training. One of the more famous names attached to this program is that of Jean Harris. Sentenced to Bedford Hills for killing her lover, Harris spent many of her years in prison helping inmates in this program. She was released in 1993.

If we do not stop the rising crime rate for women in the United States, law officials say we will be raising a whole new generation of homeless, often drug-abusing children, especially in the poorest neighborhoods. AIDS, acquired immune deficiency syndrome, can be added to the list of social problems resulting from a high female crime rate, as this fatal disease spreads fastest among drug needle users.

For a look at the reality of women in prison, in 1996, the television show *20/20* sent news correspondent Diane Sawyer behind bars. She spent two days and two nights as one of 637 prisoners in the Louisiana Correctional Institute for Women. It was an eye-opening experience for her and her audience.

When Sawyer entered the prison, her purse was checked for weapons and drugs. Normally, the new inmate must also give up everything personal, even hair spray, since it has alcohol and someone might drink it. Then comes the body search for hidden drugs, which Sawyer was spared.

Diane Sawyer was to spend her two nights in jail in the maximum security building called Capricorn. She was given a prison jumpsuit and gloves with which to clean

her eight by eight foot cell, which had a metal plate for a mirror.

The noise was deafening. There was endless shouting and banging on the bars. In maximum security, 72 women are confined to these small cells for 23 out of 24 hours. Women spend time in Capricorn for breaking the rules. One inmate broke so many rules at LCI that she spent 11 years in Capricorn.

Unlike the others, Sawyer was free to roam with her camera so that she could talk to the prisoners. One-third of all the inmates were in for drug possession, a much higher rate than the males. One woman has been at LCI for 24 years, more than any other inmate. She robbed a store with some men and pulled the trigger on a gun. She was 16 at the time. The youngest prisoner at LCI is just

The majority of women in prison are mothers of children under the age of 18. Some prisons, like Sing Sing, have facilities to care for these children. As part of their rehabilitation, mothers in prison are taught the parenting skills they may not have learned on the outside.

Diane Sawyer spent 2 days behind bars for a 20/20 report in 1996. During her stay at the Louisiana Correctional Facility for Women, Sawyer experienced the harsh realities of prison life: cramped living conditions, no privacy, and overwhelming loneliness.

17. She was with her boyfriend when he shot a woman and her son, strangers to them. They were both convicted of manslaughter. She is in for 50 years.

Sawyer learned that the women form play families in prison, calling themselves, mom, dad, kids. Some of this play acting is done for protection from others.

Most of the prisoners talk about loneliness. In the middle of more than 600 women, they say the loneliness can be unbearable.

The prison warden told Sawyer that 50 percent of the inmates don't really need to be behind bars. They should be in community programs, mainly for drug abuse. When she asked him how many of the women will be back after they are paroled, the warden said as many of 70 to 80 percent. He thinks it's because prison teaches them that they are failures and there is no way out.

Sawyer left the prison after her two-day stay with a lot of camera footage and some sobering thoughts on life behind bars. And she is free. For the others, when freedom comes they will take along $10, a bus ticket, and three strikes against them.

We know that the percentage of women in jail in the United States is on the rise. And we know that the main reason for incarceration of women is drug use and related crimes, such as stealing money to sustain the drug habit. It would seem to make sense that we concentrate on drug rehab programs in women's prisons. Unfortunately, most prisons have not caught up with this concept yet. Most female offenders get little drug rehab behind bars, and even fewer are admitted to residential aftercare programs. What is the point, critics say, of locking up someone for drug abuse and then ignoring any form of treatment?

The Youthful Offender

A Youthful Offender, or YO, is a person who is between 16 and 18 years old at the time he or she commits a crime. Age distinguishes the YO from a JO, a juvenile offender. A JO is a person who commits an offense at age 14 or 15. To be tried as a YO, the conviction must be in a local criminal court and the accused must have no prior criminal convictions.

If the youth has a prior felony conviction or if the present conviction is for a violent crime such as murder or an armed felony, he or she may be tried as an adult. You have probably heard of cases where the crime has been so horrendous—for example, a teenager shoots three schoolmates in the schoolyard—that the prosecution asks for the case to be tried in adult court. If that happens, the offender is in for a harder time.

For any young person caught up in the criminal justice system, there are definite advantages to being tried as a YO instead of an adult. No matter the crime,

Children who commit crimes when they are between the ages of 16 and 18 are classified as Youthful Offenders. The YO's criminal record is sealed, and known only by the probation and parole departments. Judges also have more freedom in sentencing a YO, which means he or she may receive more lenient sentences than an adult who commits the same crime.

the judge does not have to send the YO to prison. And if prison is the outcome, the stay will be shorter than for an adult committing the same crime.

Another very big plus when tried as a YO is that the case records are sealed. Only under extraordinary circumstances can a previous YO offense be used against a repeat offender even if he or she is now an adult. That information, however, is shared with parole and probation departments. Oddly enough, in some states the records of a juvenile offender, who is younger than a YO, are not sealed.

An exception to the sealed records is the military. The U.S. military does not recognize this YO exemption. So, if a convicted YO later wants to join the navy, for instance, he or she might well be turned down.

Years ago, many people felt that a young criminal was just the kid next door gone wrong. That is not likely to be true today. Teens, even preteens, are often seen as more of a danger, more of a threat to serene life in the community, than adult offenders. Kids seem less in control of themselves, less likely to think of the consequences of their actions. They are more likely to commit random acts of violence. The outbreak of school shootings in the late 1990s seems to support that contention.

Indeed, violence has become very much a part of the juvenile world. Prior to the 1980s, young people were most likely to die in car accidents or from suicide. During the 1980s, teenage males of all races and cultures were more likely to die from a bullet than natural causes! Between the mid-1980s and mid-1990s, the number of U.S. children killed by guns jumped a terrifying 144 percent!

Perhaps even more startling is the rise in crimes committed by the female JO or YO. From 1989 to the mid-1990s, arrests of juvenile girls more than doubled that for males—23 percent versus 11 percent. The rates of crime for young men, however, are still substantially higher than for young women. Female youths were involved in six percent of arrests for murder, 18 percent for assault, and 31 percent for theft.

After being convicted, a female YO or JO is less likely to be taken from her home than is her male counterpart. She is more likely to be given a sentence that requires home detention.

The worst school disaster in U.S. history occurred in April 1999 in Littleton, Colorado, a suburb of Denver. Two teenage students used guns and fire bombs to kill and injure some 25 of their classmates. How can these things happen? It's too easy to say it's because more weapons are more easily available, although that's true. Sociologists have a lot of theories. They cite racism, poverty, and increased violence in the movies and on television, as well as increased drug use and drug trafficking. We live in a world where the everything of the "haves" is constantly paraded before the nothing of the "have nots."

These theories may all be true, but they don't solve the problem of the youthful criminal. And the increase in crimes by young people has brought an expected reaction from older people. Overall, violent acts, homicides, and shootings in school may actually be low, but they are frequent and visible enough to send the adult world into an uproar.

Jack King of the National Association of Criminal Defense Lawyers said in an interview, "People feel outraged because they work till they drop to send their kids to college, and some YOs are given every-thing for nothing with *their* tax money. Of course, they don't think of the money we spend when we pour funds into punishment for YOs instead of rehabilitation."

But if citizens do not, many states do think about rehabilitation as an answer for the crimes of the YO and JO. Over the past 20 years, states such as Arkansas, Hawaii, Massachusetts, Missouri, Montana, and Utah have been trying a more balanced approach to juvenile crime. They wanted programs that would hold young people accountable for their deeds but would also give them the opportunity to develop productive lives.

Most juvenile prisons or training schools in the United States are large institutions housing large numbers of offenders. In circumstances involving a generally troubled population, security and discipline are big problems. The problem was so big in Washington, D.C. that YOs were chained to their desks in the classroom so they couldn't run away. In Idaho, 13-year-olds were made to stand with their noses to the wall for hours if they broke a rule. In Florida, kids as young as 10 years were sometimes thrown into isolation cells for as long as 60 days.

There just had to be a better way. Large-scale institutions did not seem to be working. So some states, like Utah and Massachusetts, decided to replace them with smaller facilities that would provide more educational and treatment options for the individual youth.

In the 1980s, Utah closed its 166-bed Youth Development Center because one out of every four YOs who left the center went back to crime. It seemed as though what Utah was teaching in prison was how to be a good criminal, not how to be a good citizen.

In place of the old structure, the state built two 30-bed facilities. Each YO had a private bedroom. In groups of 10, they ate meals together and shared a common living room area. Drug treatment and family counseling were available, as was therapy for the sex offender. Education was stressed and encouraged. After a four-year study, the rate of those who returned to crime had dropped by 70 percent.

Utah isn't Utopia, of course. It still has lots of problems with YOs. In fact, state officials lengthened the sentences for some of its YOs in the 1990s in

response to the people's demand for a crackdown on teen violence. So, smaller facilities and more personal attention may not be the whole answer, but it's better than it was.

The State of Massachusetts is often cited as a model in treatment of its youthful offenders. In 1970, it closed all of its large juvenile institutions and built 14 small ones around the state, each with 15 to 30 beds.

Public condemnation of the YO grows as violent crimes committed by children, like school shootings, become more visible and sensationalized by the media. Although the general public may disagree, many states support rehabilitation programs aimed at the youthful offender.

About 15 percent of the state's YOs, those with violent tendencies, live in these locked facilities where they receive special programs and attention. Nonviolent YOs in Massachusetts live in group homes under intensive supervision. If they respond well, they are given more freedom and responsibility. If they do not respond or do not obey the rules, they are given more restrictions.

For both the violent and nonviolent YOs, the response has been encouraging. In Massachusetts, the youth who has served time in one of these places is less likely to return to crime than in other states. Again, it's not a miracle cure, but it does seem to be working. And although Massachusetts initially spent more money than other states to develop this program, it now saves about $11 million a year in treating its YOs.

Other states have tried different ways to deal with the horrendous problem of juvenile crime and lost lives. Ohio (Cleveland), Colorado (Denver), and Alabama (Mobile) experimented with juvenile boot camps. Intended for nonviolent offenders under the age of 18, the camps last for three months at one residence, followed by six months of care in the community. The idea is to improve educational skills over the three-month period. Although most of the YOs did improve in reading, spelling, and math, the overall results of the camps were disappointing. They did not cut down on the number of YOs who returned to crime.

The Office of Juvenile Justice and Delinquency Prevention (OJJDP), which is part of the Department of Justice, thinks that the way to stop violent and chronic child offenders is to prevent them from getting that way in the first place. And the way to do that is to strengthen the four institutions that most influence young people: family, social institutions, community programs, and peer groups. OJJDP recommends more state support for single mothers and good available

Large-scale institutional settings do not seem to work in rehabilitating the youthful offender. Some states have tried programs like boot camps, which emphasize educational training and discipline in smaller groups.

daycare, especially for poor people. Schools, churches, and community organizations should get involved and help devise programs to keep kids occupied and off the streets. Schools should provide peer group counseling and community volunteer service.

On a state level, the city of New Haven, Connecticut, is an example of an all-out effort to do something about the climate of violence that surrounds young people. The Child Development-Community Policing (CD-CP) Program brings together police officers and mental health professionals. It has become a model for such cooperation across the country.

The CD-CP was formed as a result of a growing level of neglect and violence involving children throughout the 1990s. About 2 1/2 million young people, ages 12 to 17, were victims of crime in America during one year. More than three million cases of child neglect were reported to public welfare agencies. Forty-five percent of inner city schoolchildren said they were threatened with a gun. Among African-American young men ages 15 to 24, the leading cause of death is homicide. One out of ten children seen in a Boston hospital reported that they had witnessed a shooting or stabbing either in the street or at home.

For those kids already in trouble, the statistics are even worse. In a survey of YOs in detention in New York City, 79 percent had seen someone stabbed or shot, and 38 percent had been stabbed or shot themselves! Of 30 YOs held in Connecticut, 83 percent said they had seen a shooting and 63 percent said they had been shot!

These are shocking statistics. Police and mental health professionals are especially worried—and with good reason—that these children who see so much violence will in turn become violent themselves. To improve this situation, New Haven's CD-CP program has five strategies: (1) police officers go through Child Development Fellowships, spending three to four months learning how to recognize the early signs of trouble in children and their families; (2) mental health professionals spend time with the police on patrols so that they come to understand the kinds of lives these children lead and the problems that confront the police in dealing with them; (3) over a 10-week period each year, seminars are held on child development for the police, mental health professionals, and probation officers; (4) a consultation service is set up so that police in the neighborhood have a place to report possible troubles or difficult situations; and (5) the staff of the CD-CP program meets weekly to discuss the difficult cases reported by the neighborhood police.

These strategies seem to be working in New Haven. Juvenile crime is down and, just as important, recidivism is down. The New Haven program even seems to have an effect on truancy. In just the first six months that volunteers began canvassing neighborhoods with follow-up visits to the homes, unexcused absences from school dropped by 20,000! That alone reduces the petty kind of crime that some youngsters commit while hiding out during school hours.

New Haven's CD-CP model has been successful enough for other states to take interest. Programs are now underway in Charlotte, North Carolina; Nashville, Tennessee; and Portland, Oregon.

The state and the federal governments are not alone in their concern over rising youth crime. In most European countries, for instance, YO crimes have risen sharply through the 1990s. In England and Wales in the mid-1980s, about 360 out of every 100,000 teens ages 14 to 16 were convicted or charged with violent crimes. By the mid-1990s, that figure was 580 for every 100,000. Juvenile-on-juvenile crimes also increased. In The Netherlands, for instance, teens 15 to 17 were four times more likely than adults to be victims of assault.

The justice system regards a juvenile as 14 or 15 years old. Most people think that age 14 is pretty young to be committing any sort of crime, but sociologists think the problem begins much earlier, perhaps in infancy. A troubled home life can produce a troubled baby who may grow into a troubled juvenile, and so on. That's why prevention is so important. If it works, it not only saves our youths and their families, but it's a lot easier and cheaper than dealing with the more serious problems that may develop.

Once the serious problems have begun, however,

Many experts believe the best way to reduce the number of youth crimes is to get involved with children before they get involved in criminal activity. Programs that educate young people and get them involved in their community have been show to reduce the number of children committing crimes.

is there light at the end of the rehabilitation tunnel? One New York City social worker thinks so. She says the answer is personal intervention with each YO. She is especially proud of one case involving a youth of 14 who was part of a gang that committed a particularly horrendous attack on a young woman in a park a number of years ago. Although he did not actually take part in the crime, just being there was enough to send him to jail. But the social workers got through to him. Today, he is 24 years old, has finished college, and holds a responsible job in the city.

Actual statistics of how many YOs turn out like that young man are hard to come by since records are usually sealed. If a JO or YO gets to be 19 and commits a crime, we do not know if he or she has a previous record and is a repeat offender. If, however, a young person who is being monitored is in school, is working, is settled in the community, and has not committed another crime, we do know that. Says the social worker, "If rehabilitation is done seriously and well, the program really works with young offenders. They come out better than they went in."

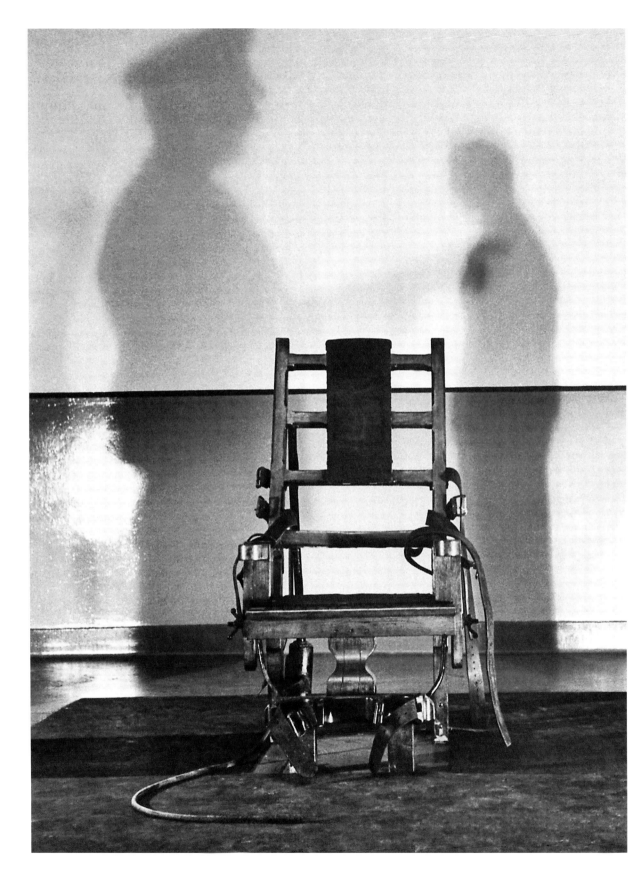

THE DEATH
PENALTY

The merit of the death penalty as the ultimate form of punishment has been debated throughout the history of the United States. To its supporters, it represents justice and retribution for heinous crimes. To its detractors, it represents society's failure to rehabilitate the criminal.

I n the United States, the death penalty dates back to colonial days. Following the harsh British codes, death was generally accepted as just punishment for a number of offenses. However, the Quakers in South Jersey did not permit capital punishment at all, and William Penn's Pennsylvania colony limited it to punishment for treason and murder.

Not everyone else was in agreement on this issue. From the very beginning of the death penalty debate, those for and against capital punishment argued about the merits—both morally and practically—of death as punishment and/or deterrent. Through the years, public opinion and public policy have gone back and forth over the issue. Since this is a state-by-state issue, it is almost necessary to keep a score card to know where capital punishment is legal. For instance, after the Civil War ended in 1865, the State of Maine abolished the death penalty. But almost immediately, the state legislature made it legal again—until 1887. Today, the death penalty is still off the books in Maine.

Early in the twentieth century, reform-minded leaders once again called for the end of the death penalty. By 1917, nine states and Puerto Rico had outlawed it. But by 1921, five of those states made it legal again. Then came the Prohibition Era of the 1920s and early 1930s, which nearly killed the drive for abolishing capital punishment. Alcohol was outlawed by the Eighteenth Amendment to the U.S. Constitution, which created the "bootlegger," a new kind of criminal who dealt in the transporting and selling of illegal alcohol. Bootlegging led to notorious gang wars and murders, and a feeling that lawlessness had taken over the nation's streets gripped the public. Few people were in a "let's be lenient to criminals" frame of mind. Prohibition was repealed by the Twenty-first Amendment in 1933, but between 1917 and 1957, no state changed its existing death penalty law. A few years later, sentiment began to swing to the other side as the Civil Rights movement took hold.

Through the years, even those against capital punishment had generally accepted the fact that it was legal according to the U.S. Constitution. However, in 1972 trial of *Furman v. Georgia*, the U.S. Supreme Court ruled that the death penalty was "cruel and unusual punishment" under the Eighth Amendment. This amendment, part of the original Bill of Rights added to the Constitution in 1791, states: excessive bail shall not be required, nor excessive fines imposed, nor cruel and unusual punishments inflicted."

The Furman case concerned a African American man convicted of murder in Georgia, and the jury sentenced him to death. In a five to four decision, the Court found that the death penalty was imposed in this, and other jury decisions, in an arbitrary way with no guidelines as to how such a decision was reached. The majority of the Court ruled that this random pattern of imposing the death penalty was cruel and unusual punishment. In effect, the Court said that without specific guidelines to impose the death penalty, a person could be executed in one place but not another for committing the same crime, which constitutes cruel and unusual punishment. Furthermore, argued the judges, death as punishment was more frequently applied to the poor and socially disadvantaged — an argument still heard today. Again, this irrational use made the punishment cruel and unusual.

As a result of the *Furman* decision, executions came to a halt in all 39 states that had the death penalty. That decision affected some 600 people on Death Row. But just when it seemed to opponents of capital punishment that their cause was gaining ground, the Supreme Court handed down another meaningful decision. In *Gregg v. Georgia* (1976), the Court upheld the death penalty in the sentencing of a man convicted of murder and armed robbery. The vote was 7 to 2. The Court declared that in this case the death penalty was not cruel and unusual punishment because the State of Georgia had provided guidelines to the jury before the sentencing. In effect, the Court said that the death penalty, according to the Constitution, was legal.

Many people feel that such court decisions have muddied the waters concerning capital punishment. The pendulum swings back and forth, but the trend at the beginning of the twenty-first century favors the pro-capital punishment side. Thirty eight states presently allow the death penalty, although some, such as New York State, have not held an execution in well over a quarter of a century. Twelve states—Alaska, Hawaii, Iowa, Maine, Massachusetts, Michigan, Minnesota, North Dakota, Rhode Island, Vermont, West Virginia, and Wisconsin — as well as Washington, D.C., have no capital punishment.

There may never be total agreement on this issue. As society calls for the death penalty for certain crimes, we are sending the message that we have given up on rehabilitating certain people. One related case does pose an interesting question about how serious we, as a society, are about rehabilitating people. It involves Karla Faye Tucker.

The debate over the death penalty has polarized the United States, and there may never be complete agreement on this issue. Instances like Karla Faye Tucker's death row rehabilitation fuel both sides of the argument: some saw her rehab as sincere, while others believed she was merely trying to avoid her execution.

Her crime made sensational news. In 1983, Tucker, a 23-year-old drug addict, and her boyfriend, Daniel Ryan Garrett, axed to death her former boyfriend, Jerry Lynn Dean, and his companion, Deborah Thornton, while they were sleeping. There was little doubt of her guilt. In fact, at her trial, she seemed rather proud of her actions.

Tucker and Garrett were sentenced to death, but he died in prison of liver disease. In various pleas to save her life, Tucker's lawyers argued that the now 38-year-old woman was a totally different person than the one who had committed such horrible acts 15 years earlier. Although she admitted her guilt, she had now found religion, had a spotless behavior record behind bars, and obviously seemed to have been rehabilitated. Tucker wrote to Texas Governor George W. Bush that the murders were "the most horrible nightmare of my life" and that she was no longer a threat to society. She asked her sentence to be changed to life imprisonment, which would have made her eligible for parole in 2003.

On February 3, 1998, Karla Faye Tucker was put to death in the state of Texas by lethal injection. She was the first woman executed in the United States since 1984, the year she was convicted. Those who agree with the execution say that religious conversions in prisons are all too common and are not a legitimate reason to change a sentence. Governor Bush refused to spare her life. He said that he could only consider whether there was doubt over her guilt, which there wasn't, or whether she had had a fair trial, which she did.

Why didn't the State of Texas lift the death penalty for Karla Faye Tucker Brown, who married a prison chaplain while behind bars? No one can know for sure, of course, but it does seem as though Tucker was rehabilitated. Isn't that what so many of us claim we want?

WHERE DO WE GO FROM HERE?

Where do we go from here? How are we doing in our efforts to stop crime, to discourage recidivism, to see if we can make rehabilitation really work?

We aren't the only ones to be asking such questions as these. Janet Reno, attorney general of the United States, and the U.S. Congress are asking, too. So is the National Institute of Justice.

Everyone probably agrees that our first priority should be stopping crime. If we do that, we really don't have to worry about all the other stuff like trials and jails and the death penalty. But how do we do that?

Perhaps one way is to see if our efforts at rehabilitation are working. These four case histories may give us some idea. The stories are true, although the names and

Many supporters of rehabilitation believe that the best way to stop crime is to educate the criminal. If a criminal has the resources that education and job training provide, he or she may be less likely to commit another crime.

some of the nonessential facts have been changed.

Case 1: John K. murdered a man and went to prison on a 15-year-to-life sentence. He was a model prisoner and took part in all the rehabilitation programs offered. His conduct got him a parole after 15 years. Before prison, John had been a railroad conductor. Naturally, he couldn't go back to that job and it was difficult to find another. Prospective employers, of course, wanted to know where he had been the past 15 years. An ex-con is not required to divulge his past unless specifically asked if he has ever been convicted of a crime.

John's caring parole counselor noticed one day that he was wearing an expensive looking leather belt. When asked about it, John said he had been taught leather work in prison and that he made belts for a hobby, sometimes selling one or two at a flea market. The counselor was able to get John a job in a small leather goods factory. He did so well that today he is a partner in the company and working hard to take care of his wife and two young children.

Case 2: Paula got caught for drug possession and went to jail. Vowing that she would get clean and come out to take care of her seven-year-old daughter, who was now in the care of Paula's mother, she entered the drug rehab program in prison and was eventually released on parole. Her counselor found her a job at the local YWCA where she eventually worked her way up to head of the maintenance crew. Things were looking up for Paula . . . until one night when the Y caught on fire and nearly burned down. The investigation led to Paula and the disclosure that she was back on drugs and had accidentally started a fire in the Y when she was high and supposed to be working. The Y leaders admitted that they hadn't known Paula was an ex-con, but said that wouldn't discourage them from hiring others in the future. As for Paula, she's back in jail and her daughter is back with her grandmother.

Case 3: Lyle M. went to prison for drug dealing. Like Paula, he vowed to get clean and entered the prison drug program. Before prison, he had been an auto parts salesman. Once paroled, his counselor got him a job in the same industry. Lyle worked hard, attended evening drug rehab programs, married, and settled down. Once off parole, he was able to get a tractor trailer license. Today, he owns his own rig as well as his own house where he lives with his wife and three children.

Case 4: At the age of 17, Zack J. stabbed a 16-year-old girl to death in a jealous rage. In prison, he was encouraged to get his high school diploma, which he did, and also took computer courses. He was out on parole at age 19. His parole counselor had high hopes for the handsome Zack and encouraged him to start college classes. Zack got a job in the office of the local community college and attended classes at night. All was going well until a college student was killed on campus one night, stabbed 64 times. The investigation led back to Zack, and Zack is back in prison, this time facing perhaps worse than life imprisonment.

What can these four cases tell us? Why, seemingly, did rehab work for John and Lyle, but not for Paula and Zack? We might say that both John and Lyle were highly motivated, that John was given an opportunity to do work that he truly liked, and that Lyle continued with drug rehab on the outside. Surely, these were factors. The fact that Paula was not given continuing drug treatment points out what prison officials have long known—drug rehab doesn't work if it's not extended past the prison sentence.

What about Zack? It seems obvious that Zack needed far more than prison rehabilitation. He is probably a very sick young man, but could he have been helped?

Even though lawmakers, law officials, the courts, and society have wide differences of opinion over the worth and value of rehabilitation, it seems obvious that we must give some kind of rehab a try. Our prisons are overcrowded. Building more can't be the whole answer. And even if we do build more, eventually most of the prisoners are going to get out. If they haven't been rehabilitated in some way, they will just be better criminals than when they went in.

As the twenty-first century opens, society in America may have to decide better ways to balance the scales of

Case studies and statistics show that rehabilitation programs, like the inmate GED program shown here, have been inconsistent in lowering the rate of recidivism. Some work, but some do not.

justice. Do we put more effort and money into finding rehabilitation programs that work and why they work? Or do we take a closer look, for example, at the policies of former Governor George W. Bush of Texas?

As Bush began his campaign for the presidential nomination in 1999, reporters scrutinized his record as governor. In his 1994 race against then Governor Ann Richards, Bush complained that she was soft on crime and he would get tougher. So, he did. As governor of Texas, he presided over the nation's largest prison-building program and the most number of executions. For every

100,000 people in Texas, 724 are in prison. Bush also opposed gun-control laws and wanted Texas to have liberal rights to carry guns.

It's true that crime rates have fallen in Texas. Opponents of the get tough policy, however, say that the real reasons are an improved economy, better police work, changing attitudes about crime among young people, and reduced use of crack. And experts on crime claim that there is a widespread decline in crime rates. That makes it less likely that any one policy can be given the credit.

Most everyone knows what we want to do about crime in society—keep it low and keep the streets safe. We know what we want to do, but as yet we just don't know how to do it—not completely anyway.

Further Reading

Hjelmeland, Andy. *Prisons: Inside the Big House.* Minneapolis: Lerner, 1996.

Kosof, Anna. *Prison Life in America.* New York: Watts, 1984.

Loeb, Robert. *Crime and Capital Punishment.* New York: Watts, 1986.

Oliver, Marilyn Tower. *Prisons: Today's Debate.* Hillside, NJ: Enslow, 1997.

Owens, Lois Smith. *Think About Prisons and the Criminal Justice System.* New York: Walker, 1992.

Weiss, Ann E. *Prisons: A System in Trouble.* Hillside,NJ: Enslow 1988.

Index

Index

Index

Picture Credits

ROSE BLUE, an author and educator, has written more than 70 books, both fiction and nonfiction, for young readers. Her books have appeared as TV specials and have won many awards. A native New Yorker, she lives in the Borough of Brooklyn because, as she says, she likes it!

CORINNE J. NADEN, former U.S. Navy journalist and children's book editor, also has more than 70 books to her credit. A freelance writer, she lives in Tarrytown, New York, where she shares living quarters with her two cats, Tigger and Tally Ho!

AUSTIN SARAT is William Nelson Cromwell Professor of Jurisprudence and Political Science at Amherst College, where he also chairs the Department of Law, Jurisprudence and Social Thought. Professor Sarat is the author or editor of 23 books and numerous scholarly articles. Among his books are *Law's Violence, Sitting in Judgment: Sentencing the White Collar Criminal*, and *Justice and Injustice in Law and Legal Theory*. He has received many academic awards and held several prestigious fellowships. He is President of the Law & Society Association and Chair of the Working Group on Law, Culture and the Humanities. In addition, he is a nationally recognized teacher and educator whose teaching has been featured in the *New York Times*, on the *Today* show, and on National Public Radio's *Fresh Air*.